W9-BJR-302

921
Seq

Petersen, David.

Sequoyah, father of
the Cherokee alphabet

Cil

DATE DUE

SEQUOYAH
Father of the Cherokee Alphabet

SEQUOYAH
Father of the Cherokee Alphabet

By David Petersen

CHILDRENS PRESS®
CHICAGO

PHOTO CREDITS

Project Editor: E. Russell Primm III
Design and Electronic Composition: Biner Design
Photo Research: Judith Feldman

Library of Congress Cataloging-in-Publication Data

Petersen, David
    Sequoyah (father of the Cherokee alphabet) / by David Petersen.
    p. cm. — (Picture story biography)
    Summary: A biography of the native American who gave his people the gift of reading and writing by creating the Cherokee syllabary.
    ISBN 0-516-04180-0
    1. Sequoyah, 1770?–1843 — Juvenile literature. 2. Cherokee Indians — Biography — Juvenile literature. 3. Cherokee Indians — Writing — Juvenile literature. [1. Sequoyah, 1770?–1843. 2. Cherokee Indians — Biography. 3. Indians of North America — Biography.] I. Title. II. Series: Picture-story biographies.

E99.C5S387 1991   91-13313
973'.0497502 — dc20   CIP
[B]   AC

Sequoyah accomplished much during his long life. He was a skilled silversmith, a talented painter, and an experienced soldier. He is remembered best, however, for giving his people the gift of reading and writing. Sequoyah is the only person known to have developed a writing system.

This picture of Sequoyah holding his syllabary is the most famous image of the great man.

The Smoky Mountains in Tennessee were home to the young Sequoyah.

Sequoyah was probably born about 1770, at a Cherokee village called Tuskegee. It is in the Smoky Mountains, in present-day Tennessee. Even though he is one of the greatest Cherokee heroes, Sequoyah was only half Indian.

Wuh-teh, Sequoyah's mother, was from a respected and noble Cherokee family, the Red Paint clan. They were well-known for their knowledge of their people's history. Sequoyah's father was a *unaka*, or white man.

Historians think that Sequoyah's father was most probably Nathaniel Gist. He was a friend of George Washington. He was also a hunter, explorer, and trader among the Indians.

About the time that Sequoyah was born, Nathaniel Gist left the Cherokee people. Young Sequoyah grew up without a father and was branded a "half-breed."

Sequoyah's father, Nathaniel Gist, was a famous Indian trader and friend to George Washington. Here, Gist and Washington visit an Indian village.

This Cherokee cabin in Tennessee is similar to the one Sequoyah and his mother, Wuh-teh, lived in.

During his life, Sequoyah had several names. When he was born, a sparrow landed on the window of Wuh-teh's house. She named her son Tsis-kwa'ya ("The Sparrow").

As the boy grew older other Cherokees noticed that he was lame in one leg. This may have been caused by a disease or by an accident. No one knows for sure. The name Sequoyah means "The Lame One" in the Cherokee language.

Sequoyah also had an English name, George Guess. This is probably a misspelling of his father's name, "Gist."

As a boy Sequoyah was shy and quiet. He never went to school. Other Cherokee boys played ceremonial ball games. These games were thought to prepare the boys for war. Sequoyah preferred to sit in the woods and draw. He was fifteen when he realized how rewarding drawing could be. He also

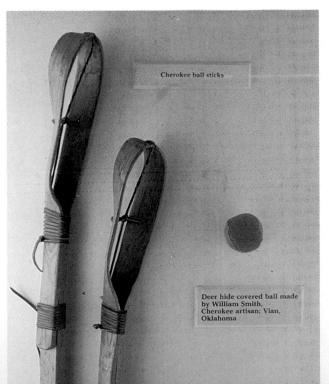

Cherokee ball sticks

Deer hide covered ball made by William Smith, Cherokee artisan; Vian, Oklahoma

Ceremonial ball games were an important part of Cherokee boyhood. They were thought to be preparation for war. Sequoyah preferred to paint and draw.

enjoyed using his hands and tools. He built furniture and small buildings for his mother.

Sequoyah discovered that he was very good at detailed work. When he was about twenty years old he began working with silver. He soon was a skilled silversmith. His work was often decorated with designs of birds and animals. Sequoyah traveled around North and South Carolina, Georgia, and Alabama selling his work. While in Alabama he learned how to be a blacksmith.

Sequoyah was very talented at using tools in silver making, blacksmithing, and art. Cherokees today continue the tradition of fine handworked art.

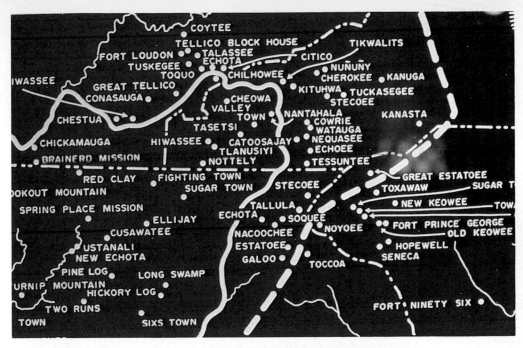

Before being moved west by the U.S. government, the Cherokees lived in the areas of present day Tennessee, Georgia, and North and South Carolina. This map shows Cherokee towns of the 1700 and 1800s.

Sequoyah settled in a house that he built on the Coosa River near Willstown, Alabama. He worked as a blacksmith and married a woman named Utiya from a nearby Cherokee town. Sequoyah and Utiya had four boys. Sequoyah's business was good and the towns people respected him.

When the Creek Indian War began many Cherokee men joined the U.S. Army. On October 13, 1813, Sequoyah also joined. He fought under Andrew Jackson at the Battle of Horseshoe Bend. He was discharged in April 1814.

Several years before the war, Sequoyah had found a new interest. At the age of thirty-nine, Sequoyah found

A copy of Sequoyah's army record under the name George Guess

the "talking leaves." These were the pieces of paper with written words. The white man used them to send messages to each other. Sequoyah's discovery changed his life forever. It also changed the lives of every Cherokee man, woman, and child.

The "talking leaves" were on Sequoyah's mind all during the Creek Indian War. He began to think how nice it would be if his children could learn to read and write. If only there were a Cherokee alphabet!

At this time, the Cherokees had no written language. Any Cherokee who wanted to read and write had to learn English. Because very few Cherokee people had the opportunity to learn English, most of them remained illiterate.

Well, Sequoyah thought, if white people can send messages to one another on paper then why couldn't Indians do the same? He believed they could, and he would prove it.

At first, Sequoyah tried to invent a picture symbol for every word in the Cherokee language. But soon he realized there were too many words for each one to have its own symbol. Instead, Sequoyah tried to make a symbol for each of the sounds in the Cherokee language. This was much more practical.

Sequoyah spent years listening to the Cherokee language and finding the individual syllables. Finally he identified eighty-six separate sounds. When these eighty-six sounds were put together in different combinations, they formed all of the words in the Cherokee language.

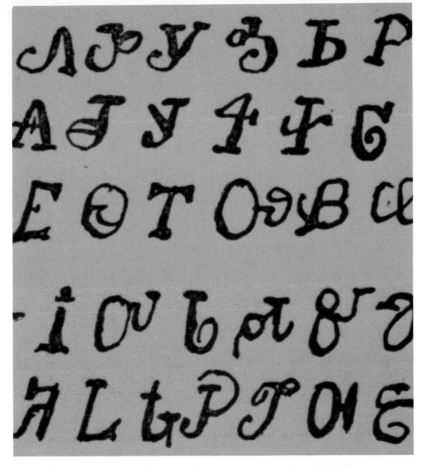

Sequoyah's work toward a written language for the Cherokee allowed his people to communicate with one another over the long distances that separated his people.

Next Sequoyah needed to design a character to represent each of these sounds. He designed a simple character to represent each of them. Some of these characters he borrowed from the English alphabet. Others he took from ancient languages, such as Greek and Hebrew. Still others he created himself. He carved his figures on the smooth insides of slabs of tree bark. This was the closest thing to paper he could find. Sequoyah had invented a syllabary.

How is a syllabary different from an alphabet? An alphabet uses symbols to represent letters —A, B, C, and so on — for the twenty-six letters in the English alphabet. The letters are then combined in various ways to make words.

A syllabary uses symbols to stand for sounds. We can use Sequoyah's name to illustrate the difference between an alphabet and a syllabary.

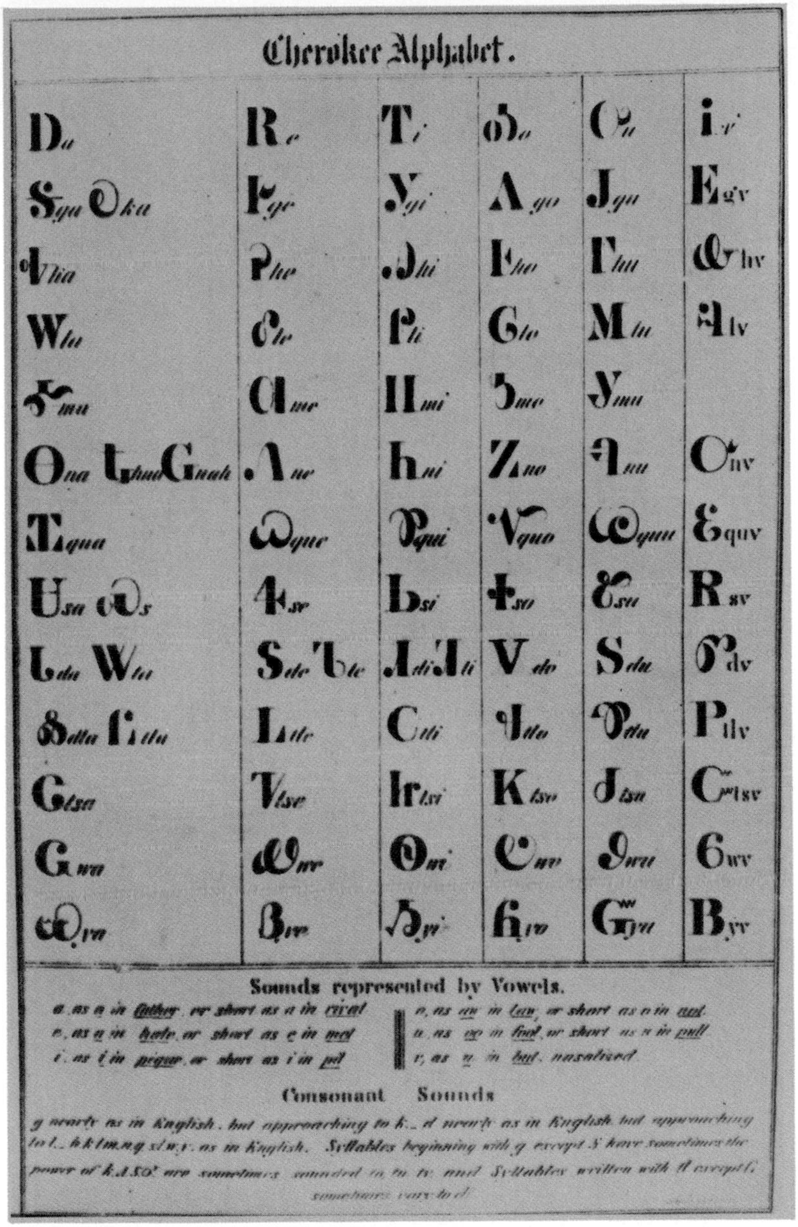

An early printed example of Sequoyah's syllabary

In the English alphabet, the name "Sequoyah" contains eight letters: S-e-q-u-o-y-a-h. But when divided into syllables, there are only three: Se-quo-yah.

Sequoyah spent twelve years perfecting the Cherokee syllabary. It was so sensible, however, that most of his students were able to learn it in just a few days.

This picture contrasts an early version of the syllabary with the final version.

The work on Sequoyah's syllabary was hard and slow. For a long time nobody believed Sequoyah would ever be able to make the leaves talk. Some neighbors whispered that he had gone crazy. Others thought he had fallen under the spell of an evil witch. Even Utiya began to doubt her husband. One day, in a rage, she threw all of her husband's work into the fire.

Sequoyah left his village. The scorn, the gossip, and the anger were too much for him. He found an old cabin several miles from his village. Sequoyah ignored the talking and teasing and kept working.

The Cherokees, however, did not ignore him. One night a group from the village came and burned the cabin to the ground. Inside was all of Sequoyah's work on his syllabary.

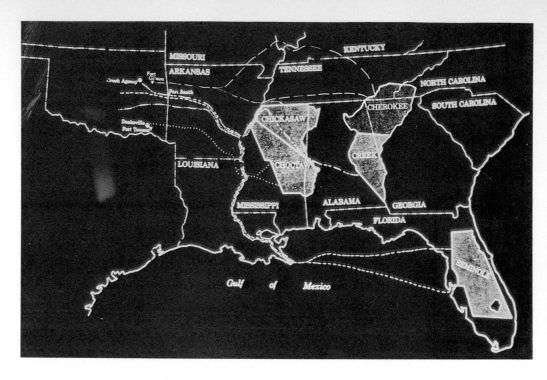

More than 4,000 Cherokees died when they were forced by the government to march westward from their homes in the Southeastern United States. Sequoyah's work allowed the separated Cherokee to communicate with each other.

Sequoyah was nearly fifty at this time. He decided to take his youngest child, Ah-yoka, and move to Arkansas. Many Cherokees had moved there; perhaps they would be more understanding.

Sequoyah and Ah-yoka joined a group of other Cherokees who were also going to Arkansas. Among the group, Sequoyah met a woman named Sally and her eight-year-old son.

Sequoyah married Sally by the time they reached Fort Smith, Arkansas. They continued and settled in Polk County. Sequoyah built a cabin for his new family and returned to his work.

Finally, in 1821, his syllabary was complete. Now he needed a student to teach it to.

This honor fell to his only daughter, Ah-yoka. Together, Sequoyah and Ah-yoka would prove that the "crazy scratching" was important.

Sequoyah and his daughter Ah-yoka

Sequoyah went to his old friend Chief John Ross. Ross was the head of the council of Cherokee chiefs. He was also a very learned man. He had gone to college at Dartmouth in New Hampshire. In college, he learned to speak many languages. These included English, French, Spanish, Latin, Greek, and of course, Cherokee. Chief Ross agreed that Sequoyah could come before the group and show his work.

Together, Sequoyah and Ah-yoka would show the usefulness of the syllabary. Sequoyah left the council house. In his absence, the chief told Ah-yoka some things to write down. When this had been done, Sequoyah was sent for. Sequoyah read what Ah-yoka had written, word for word, exactly as the chiefs had said it.

The members of the council were not convinced. They were still frightened by the talk of Sequoyah's

Chief John Ross

magic. They demanded another test to
prove what Sequoyah had done. This
time Chief Ross suggested that the
process be reversed. The council
dictated to Sequoyah, and Ah-yoka
read the words back to the council.

Finally, the council believed in what Sequoyah had done. They sat in silence. They were amazed. No longer was Sequoyah scorned as a crazy man.

The syllabary was accepted at last. Sequoyah's next task was to share it with as many of his people as he could. In 1822, Sequoyah taught hundreds of Tennessee Cherokees to read and write. He then returned to Arkansas to teach his syllabary to the Cherokee people living there. Soon, Eastern (Tennessee)

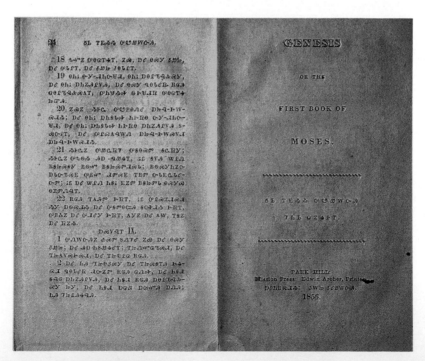

The bible was one of the first books to be translated into the Cherokee language.

Soon after the establishment of the syllabary a newspaper in Cherokee was started. At left an example of the *Cherokee Phoenix*, and at right the newspaper office.

and Western (Arkansas) Cherokees were writing each other letters.

In 1824, a young Cherokee translated part of the New Testament of the bible with the new syllabary. A year later, in 1825, the entire New Testament was translated. Soon a newspaper called the *Cherokee Phoenix* was published using the new writing system. The first issue came out on February 21, 1828, in New Echota, Georgia.

The Cherokee nation was so pleased by Sequoyah's work that it gave him a silver medal in 1824. On one side were the words, "Presented to George Gist by the General Council of the Cherokee Nation." Under these words were two crossed pipes. These represented the Eastern and Western Cherokees.

The Cherokee Nation awarded Sequoyah this silver medal for his great contribution to his people.

Sequoyah's cabin in Indian Territory

In 1829, Sequoyah and his family moved to Indian Territory. This is now the state of Oklahoma. There, they settled at a place called Skin Bayou, near present-day Sallisaw. With the help of his wife and children, Sequoyah raised livestock, grew a garden, made and sold salt, and built a one-room log cabin.

After living quietly for many years in Indian Territory, Sequoyah decided to visit Old Mexico. He hoped to find a band of Cherokee living there and teach them to read and write. His son Tessee kept him company on the long journey. They left with several other Cherokees in the summer of 1842.

But Sequoyah had waited too long to begin such a difficult journey. He was now an old man of more than seventy years. The long, hard weeks of travel soon proved too much for him. In the summer of 1843, near the Mexican village of San Fernando, Sequoyah fell ill and died.

When Oklahoma became a state in 1907, the new government sent a statue of Sequoyah to Washington, D.C., for the capitol. This was not the first tribute to the great man. In 1849, a scientist named Stephen L. Endlicher named the huge redwood trees in California after Sequoyah. And in 1890, a park named Sequoia National Park was created.

The majestic redwood trees were named Sequoias in honor of Sequoyah (left). In 1890, Sequoia National Park was also named for the great Cherokee leader.

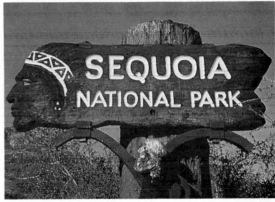

This painting of Sequoyah in traditional Cherokee dress hangs in the Oklahoma State Capitol.

Sequoyah had not had an easy life. He grew up without a father. He was called a "half-breed." His leg was lame. He was scorned as a crazy man by his own people. Yet, through hard work and strength of character, Sequoyah overcame all of these problems.

Throughout his life, Sequoyah preferred to think of himself as all Indian. He spoke only Cherokee. He never learned to read or write English, though he may have been able to understand English when he heard it. Sequoyah dressed in traditional Cherokee clothing. In every way, Sequoyah was among the greatest of the Cherokee people.

SEQUOYAH

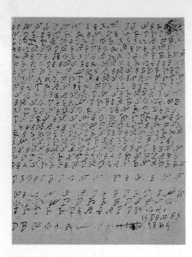

This letter, written in Cherokee by an Indian scout, informed government officials in Washington, D.C., of Sequoyah's death in Mexico.

1770 (circa)	Sequoyah born at or near the Cherokee village of Tuskegee, in the Great Smoky Mountains of present-day Tennessee.
1812?	Marries Utiya.
1813–1814	Sequoyah and other Cherokee men join American colonists in fighting the British and their allies, the Creek Indians.
1818	Sequoyah joins the Western Cherokee Nation in Arkansas; meets and marries Sally.
1821	Sequoyah's syllabary perfected and presented to the Eastern Cherokee Tribal Council.
1824	Eastern Cherokee Nation presents Sequoyah with a silver medal.
1829	Sequoyah and his family build a log cabin on their allotted ten acres in Indian Territory; the first Indian-language newspaper, *The Cherokee Phoenix*, is printed, using Sequoyah's syllabary.
1842	Sequoyah, his son Tessee, and a friend named The Worm depart for a months-long tour of Mexico, hoping to locate a band of Cherokees living there.
1843	Sequoyah, about seventy years old, dies near San Fernando, Mexico.
1849	Giant California redwood trees are named in honor of Sequoyah.
1917	Statue of Sequoyah is unveiled at the Nation's Capitol in Washington, D.C.

INDEX

ABOUT THE AUTHOR

David Petersen was raised in Oklahoma, and visited Sequoyah's homesite and cabin often. He now lives in a cabin of his own in the Colorado Rockies. He is the author of *Racks: The Natural History of Antlers and the Animals That Wear Them* (Capra Press, 1991) and a dozen or so other books.